MW00627936

MY RÍASTRAD

MY RÍASTRAD

Poems by

Kevin Hogan

Dear Dan,
of all the words
I've met so far
my best are here!
Enjoy,
1-15-16

Antrim House

Simsbury, Connecticut

Copyright © 2015 by Kevin Hogan

Except for short selections reprinted for purposes of
book review, all reproduction rights are reserved.
Requests for permission to replicate should
be addressed to the publisher.

Library of Congress Control Number: 2015941226

ISBN: 978-1-936482-86-3

First Edition, 2015

Printed & bound by United Graphics, Inc.

Book design by Rennie McQuilkin

Front cover photograph: *Minot's Ledge Lighthouse Slammed
by Nor'easter Waves,* Steve Steinmetz
(www.sjspix.com)

Celtic illustrations and author photo by Aislinge Productions

Antrim House
860.217.0023
AntrimHouse@comcast.net
www.AntrimHouseBooks.com
21 Goodrich Road, Simsbury, CT 06070

To My Gypsy

ACKNOWLEDGMENTS

Poetry may appear a solitary endeavor, but ultimately, words do not reach the page without the contributions of others. The following is a brief and by no means comprehensive list of those who've given their selfless encouragement and support.

Grateful acknowledgement to Matt Cresswell, editor of *Glitterwolf Magazine,* in which "Collect Yourself" and "The Gender Bend" first appeared.

Re-Re, we did it, darling! And Frankie would be proud. Beyond all your sacrifices, thank you for making me as much Murphy as Hogan.

Jack Smiler, you are the north star of courage and friendship. I thank my stars everyday for knowing you.

Jonny Bowden, I finally get to thank you for being as much a friend as a trusted mentor. No word from you was ever lost on me.

Philip Gordon, you reminded me that good is still worth fighting for, while laughing at the madness in the fray. You're a hero—keep crushing evil!

Carolyn McKibbin, you opened your heart as much as your mind. You have my word, I'll strive to make this world better one poem at a time.

Julia Canfield, Ellyn Ruthstrom and Don Thompson, you never flinched in the face of my adversities, and instead gave me the courage to write on. Thank you for helping me find my way home.

Rennie McQuilkin, you were the first to believe in me and my work. Thank you for being as bold as you are wise.

My gypsy, partner and soul twin, thank you for accepting these shards of glass I make, only to find the stained-glass windows within. My love for you shines through on every page.

My dear reader, how you got here does not matter half as much as where you will go after. Thank you for taking the time to read.

TABLE OF CONTENTS

PART III – FITTING ROOM

PART IV – UNDER THE INFLUENCE

PART V – THE WORLD STANDS STILL

PREFACE

I was born the only child to Irish-American Catholic parents told they'd never conceive.

I grew up a conundrum to many but not all.

I witnessed Ciaran Carson read selections of his poetry from *The Irish for No*. He made words new again.

I went home and read Thomas Kinsella's translation of the *Táin Bó Cúailnge*. I met Cú Chulainn, the Irish Achilles, and felt time and symbolism shatter inside of me.

I forgot that feeling for a long time, until life made me feel it again.

So I wrote *My Ríastrad*.

MY RÍASTRAD

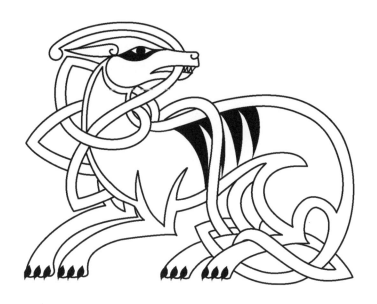

PART I

A WORD WITH YOU

FOR FRANK

Accept these few libations
For extending a hand
More than a fist,
Thereby teaching me to
Fight when it's right
And shake when not.
For this shining gem
Of judgment and so
Many more that I
Can only bring myself
To recall them slowly
One at a time,
Until on this day,
I see all your facets,
And you'll just have
To frankly forgive me
For crying out loud.

OH, WICKED ONE

On the day I should have drowned
In the ocean's lost and found
Or been crushed against a rock
By your fist, oh Hobomock,
You had other plans instead
Deep within that wicked head.
Held down by your undertow
In a world of ebb and flow,
You choked me full with spirits
Of near a hundred Irish
Who all perished within sight
Of the land of Lover's Light.
Buoyed up, I fought for shore—
Far from childhood evermore.

MAY I TROUBLE YOU

When does
A hairy experience
Become
A close shave?

When does
Grave robbing
Become
Archaeology?

When exactly does
Intelligence
Become
Artificial?

I'm a fountain
Of questions
With a drought
Of answers.

Though it's true,
I'm thankful
To trouble you.

A WORD WITH YOU

Amazing that words, just words,
Those things we use to name things,
Picked out and lined up with care
Fill books and the songs we sing.
Give a few sufficient space,
Some appropriate timing
And they might even get on
To do a bit of rhyming.
Sometimes the tender ones meet
In a whisper to the heart,
Causing a love of writing
After anger's done its part.
Explains why I'm never through
With having a word with you.

THE BULL PEN

The ritual fits
My repetitions
Like the endless stitch
On what's being pitched.

It feels good to hold
And never gets old
Once my grip is right
Between loose and tight.

Then with what I know
I wind up, let go—
And hope something's caught
Before it can drop.

That's the way I spend
Life with a bull pen.

HOMELESS IN THE METAPHOR

I still turn green with envy
At that Amherst purple sea.
Frost made them more than lucky
Through metaphors all could see.

Educations well in hand,
Plus the keys to poetry,
There was more than jobs to land
With wisdom on salary.

Though each had quite a welcome
To the literary world,
I would warn those writing home,
Be prepared the world to roam.

For your pen can leave you more
Homeless in the metaphor.

A RAIL

Departing a train,
Minutes from tourists
Queuing and photographing
The Secret Annex,
A searing jolt
Tore up my
Arm.

For my part,
I had touched
An old handrail
And was certain
It had become
Electrified by many
Volts.

The station was
In summer renovation,
And I surmised
A worker had
Let live wires
Touch the metal
Railing.

But using eyes,
And even a
Second hesitating touch,
I could find
No answer to
My surprising painful
Shock.

Months later in
A wartime archive,
I saw photos
Of star-pinned
Deportees lined up
For darkened transport
Trains.

Besides each other,
The last thing
I saw so
Many touched was
A handrail that
Would lead to
Auschwitz.

A LOVELIER WORLD

Just before sunrise,
Watching a hound
Dream of hunting,
I feel myself
Drawn to pursue
The thoughts of
A dissatisfied mind.
Cards on table,
The dog has
Never caught more
Than tennis balls,
But that doesn't
Stop him from
Envisaging furrier prey.
Comforted in camaraderie,
I bound onwards,
Straining to capture
A lovelier world
With every instinct.

THE SHADOW OF DOUBT

In the glare
Of absolute certainty,
There is right,
And, of course,
There is wrong.
And without exception,
There is no
Perception of even
One second thought.
All who persist
Become shining examples.
Must be why
I stick to
Shade in the
Shadow of doubt.

PART II

MY RÍASTRAD

SOCIAL MEDIUM

There will come a time
—If not already here—
When not a line is read
Without a monitor near.

While downloading this,
Some may compose tweets
Or check on e-mails
As the action completes.

Those with followers
Will all read this and blog
That doing just one thing
Is an impossible slog.

And in this Wi-Fi world,
All books will be for faces
With no one going anywhere
Without posting the places.

Mercifully, I am
No social medium.
Words touch me so slow
Most find it pure tedium.

SIR REALITY

In a land of make believe,
At the same time on TV,
The same knights appear nightly,
Feigning spontaneity.

Until their good King Nielsen
—Crowned in cordiality—
Raises his sceptered ratings,
Dubbing Sir Reality.

Then a large flourish is made,
As if assembling for a quest,
To gather and watch the show
That's rated to be the best.

In between commercial breaks,
Bosch and Dali laugh at fakes.

FULL CONTACT LENS

There is a game played every night—
Whether its stars know it or not.
It can fill you with such a fright,
You'll think it killed you on the spot.

In a flash, you're given a push
To trip and stumble and stammer,
Before you see it's an ambush
And you're in focus on camera.

There aren't rules, but the play begins
When they tar you in opinion,
Then you see a smile coming from
A well-trained microphoned minion.

I pray this game you never play;
But if you do, watch what you say.
Get in your car and drive away.
Your life will end—or start—that day.

PRIVACY MATTERS

Your privacy will not matter
Once the crowd stirs from its slumber,
Salivating for newstainment,
And you're served up—the taste du jour.

There are some who'll strive to question,
But there are more with opinions
Sown in fallow fields of truisms,
Perched to pluck what issues forth.

If you live to fight, you're in luck
Since most all truths split people up.
Just be warned: the more you reason,
The more you'll plant seeds for gossip.

So when the mob stings like hornets,
Close your theatres. Go write sonnets.

NO CONFIDENCE

What if you presented
The case of who you are,
Citing your body as evidence,
But when the vote comes in
It's strictly one of no confidence?

Would you change or contort
Into someone you're not?
Or would you try to make amends by
Wearing whichever mask
The voting audience recommends?

Even if your confidence
Rushed from you long ago
At speeds outstripping those of sneezes,
Take heart: you're fit to write—
Though the truth is rarely what pleases.

THE GOAT'S SONG

Long before London
Grabbed Athens' marbles
And Europa groaned
Over Hera's bills,
There were the world's first
Playbills promising
Drama escapes from
Lightweight to heavy.
Laughing or weeping,
Each mask took its hold,
Cueing the audience
To respond as told.
A goat was given
To whoever's head
Came up with the play
For which most tears were shed.
So it's far from absurd:
We're a scapegoating herd!

OFF MY CHEST

When I wake
From dead sleep
In the middle
Of the night
It nearly kills
Me with fear.
My heart knocks
Until my throat
Begins to close
And my eyes
Open to see
A sweat covered
Version of me.
Swallow a pill
Or see someone
Is the advice
I hear often
From those who
Care about me.
But with respect
To my position
I would rather
See the demons
Than suddenly awaken
One day blind
To what sits
On my chest
As I wake
From dead sleep
In the middle
Of the night.

USED TOO

I used to understand
Others better than me.
I used to stay sober
And drive all home with glee.

I used to keep the peace
While many freely flared.
I used to share my thoughts
With those who sometimes cared.

Now I face a mirror
And can see the duress
Of an old stranger's gaze
Out to end loneliness.

Just between me and you,
It's more than I am used to.

THE LAST STRAND

In a room a fathom longer than any ship,
I once observed two rope makers ply their trade,
Proud to have earned both sailors' and fishermen's trust.
By chance, I'd chosen to visit the ropewalk's final day
And witnessed the last strand being wound into place.
Along the lane in the shadow of Samuel Gray,
Rapt fibers moaned to floorboards under steel-toed shoes
Until all walking stopped, signaling hemp had become rope.
As the pair departed, I recognized both men bore
My countenance after threading words into lines of hope.
Though neither had the neck of a man who'd
Hung until the last strand broke and breathing returned,
Forever marking one with the deepest awareness of rope.

LOST AND FOUND

Ever lose something
You suspect you'll
Never get back,
And the more
You miss it,
The more it
Hurts to reminisce?
I used to
Cherish human contact.
Now I'm alone
In blinding spotlight—
Even in the
Most crowded darkroom.
So I squint,
Looking forward to
What I'll find,
Rather than turning
Back to face
What I've lost.

MY RÍASTRAD

Sétanta early felt its force
When he tore his name
And Culann's hound to pieces,
Serving later as mortal mortar
For walls of Connacht corpses.

If only Kinsella's warp spasm
And Carson's equally lethal torque
Remained Irish flights of fancy,
Echoing the chants of seanchaithe
Singing Cú Chulainn's deeds of battle,

But I've my own ríastrad
And have felt one eye
Sink inwards where no bird
Can pluck it skull-free,
Bristling outwards—a raging monster.

My frenzy stirs when those
Made victims by the weak
Are then made herded cattle
For the raiders of consumption,
Peddling fear, birth to grave.

Not unlike the Celtic hero,
My skin becomes a thornbush
And my organs twist inside
When I lay my spear
By a queen's unguarded hearth.

PART III

FITTING ROOM

FITTING ROOM

Lost halfway between
Feet and meters,
I stood holding
An Irish sweater
In the Eurozone.
A vision wearing
Stilettos and suspenders
Offered her help.
I solemnly confessed
Checking the label
Left me confused.

Setting her chin,
She proudly professed,
"Labels are shite!
It's only the
Fit that matters."

The fitting room
Gave me pause...
So many labels
Thrown like shuriken—
Stuttering punk faggot
Scribbling loner freak
Fucking fence sitter.

Making the purchase,
I heartily thanked
The sales associate,
Telling her surely,
"Go teach philosophy!"

KARMA'S A BITCH

Karma arrives, wearing
Stilettos of steel
And a gaze so hard
It can make you kneel.

If she's there for you,
Don't put up a fight.
You did something wrong;
Now she'll make it right.

No worries: she's fast—
Since there isn't a day
Without injustice
And powers at play.

So don't get huffy
If you're poor or rich,
She won't give a shit
Cause Karma's a bitch.

THE TIME OF YOUR LIFE

A shopkeeper off Socrates Street
Once handed me some change
And freely offered this advice:
Rich to poor must choose
How to spend their time,
For it will be spent
With or without their consent.
So when you're faced with
A question of some weight,
Lift your head up high,
And know that every day
You're already answering the
Question that matters most:
How will you ultimately spend
The time of your life?

LET IT GO

Lean way back
On two legs
Of a chair
Until you start
To fall backwards.

What's your reaction?

Of course, you
Reach out to
Save yourself from
Pain and impact.

Yet what if
You squandered too
Much time reaching
Out to people
Who'd prefer to
Live without you?

How long would
It take you
To lock fingers
Behind your head,
Sit tall and
Lean back on
Life, ready to
Let it go?

COLLECT YOURSELF

Reach an age.
Hold a job.
Put up fences.
Raise a family.
Give them all
Your very best,
Until the day
You wake up
In a body
As foreign as
A Kafkan bedbug.
Then as you
Lie crushed within
A thickening shell
Of external expectations,
If you discover
That you are
More than titles,
Make the journey
To where you're
Welcomed and can
Summon the strength
To smash archetypes
And the patience
To collect yourself.

YOU'RE ALL

Once your all is lost,
There is another all:
The all that sums up you
After you subtract your fall.

But while everything's up
Because you're so damn down,
Take care which way you climb—
Don't lose grip for some loose crown.

Yet when the Times are right,
There is often a voice.
I heard Ellyn Ruthstrom's
And got involved by choice.

And when you find your cause
That you would like to better,
May your welcome be as mine was
At the Bisexual Resource Center.

FRESH OUT

Who the hell
Ever thought of
Stuffing one's sexuality
Into a closet?
It gets me
So pissed off,
I run out
Of patience and
Closets to open.
Then I hear
The label lovers
Advancing for answers,
And I know
It's a damn
Good thing that
I'm fresh out!

THE ODDEST GUY

All my neighbors think I am queer
Because I shovel without fear.
When skies turn grey and fill with snow,
I dig a path from front to rear.

They start motors and make a blow
While I just smile, and on I go.
Their looks all question my mistake,
But I still wave when their cars slow.

Unlike the masses, I like ache
And wish to toil at what I make.
Not all I finish, though I try
To write—and love—for its own sake.

So view me as the oddest guy,
But I can see when others lie,
And I see them as they drive by.
Will they see me, as I am? Bi.

THE GENDER BEND

I cannot wait
For the day—
Not to mention
The night—when
The right to
Be as much
Or as little
He or she
Or any mix
Of the three
As your self
Wants to be
Is treated just
Like the freedom
To travel freely
Wherever you want.
Meanwhile, I'll be
On up ahead
With those who
Already see the
Beauty of humanity
As it curves
The gender bend.

BOSTON BI-RISH

The Irish have saints,
But I ain't one of 'em.
Boston has its Brahmins,
But don't count me among 'em.

Yet there's a cause that
Gets me so upset,
I'll face God, armies
And the belligerent.

It's a war of love
—More baked than beans—
That makes me so angry
Because it's so damn mean.

So I'll fight for a year when,
Without batting a false eyelash,
I can march with Saint Patrick
Because I'm Boston Bi-rish!

BY THE TIME

In Boston,
I've given my dedication to bi-education.
In Northampton,
I've enjoyed the brightest faces at Pride.
In Cambridge,
There's still a house that makes me party.
In Washington,
I've witnessed dashing leaders on parade.
In Uganda,
I'd be accused then jailed then killed.
In America,
I've walked across the White House lawn.

PART IV

UNDER THE INFLUENCE

PARTY SPLIT ENDS

In the United States of good locks,
We can put shampoo and conditioner
Into just one bottle, but we can't
Put two political parties into
Just one room to work together.
Yes, it's enough to make one's hair
Stand on end, except for the fact
That in the shower we have one
Product that can address the build-up
Of oil while also nurturing and
Protecting each strand of who we are—
Not to mention it discourages flakes!
It's time to release the beauticians
And give our government a brush up
So that someday, Washington will be
Tangle-free and shine just like our hair.

I'LL BE DAMNED

In battles fought
And yet to come,
Good and evil's
In everyone.
Of course, don't look
In propaganda
For this truth or
Kind of candor.
We kill over
God and money.
It's as tragic
As it's funny.
We invented
Both gods and wars.
So after church,
We march to stores,
And there we spend
As if we must,
Shopping—because
In God we trust.

HERE AFTER

Strutting and fretting
An idiot's tale,
The Scottish King
Blew his candle
To her hereafter.

Bending and praying
To selected gods,
Others put faith
In soulful gatherings
Of segregated hereafters.

Guess I'm pagan,
Striving to leave
This world pristine
For those who
Come here after.

WILD WEST

On a shelf of California
Caught between a sea of stars
And an elevated desert,
I found myself in line one day
At a bank near old gold mines
And new military fences.
The man in front of me was
Speaking Spanish on his phone,
Asking a friend to have the
Machete under his seat ready.
Apparently, someone had
Just been robbed outside
By kids with chains on bikes.
That was the last day
I ever wondered if
I'd missed the Wild West.

NATIVE AMERICA

Chief Joseph knew the earth
As a mother who played
No favorites amongst
All her equal children
Who were free to travel
Without reservations.
Later, his cause of death
Would be a broken heart.
And then when the bearded
Face of evil was found
At zero dark thirty,
Americans flew in
Apaches and Black Hawks—
Locked, loaded and ready
To be the one to yell,
For God and country,
  Geronimo,
    Geronimo,
      Geronimo!

THE WELL-DRAWN NOTEBOOK MAN

There is a man in Pyongyang town
With a big hat and bigger frown.
His job seems simple: just write down
Every word from his leader's crown.

But he's headed for some trouble
Since his pen began to double
As an agent against rubble
In his own creative bubble.

Now, not noting the need for trains,
He sketches horses with long manes
Ridden smartly down country lanes.
It's so clear! His problem remains.

Until the day there comes a plan
To erase one drawn notebook man.

GHOST ARMY

One day in the summer,
They were all delivered:
Letters in mailboxes
That made old men shiver.

Thousands of grandfathers
Held draft registrations
For their own grandfathers—
Well past their cremations.

The Selective Service
Blames clerical error
For putting families
Through this bizarre terror.

Though others claim what we're
Beginning to observe
Is the conscription of
A ghost army reserve.

1

They say there's strength in numbers,
But really, what do they know?
Sure, if you're building armies,
You want as many as will go.

From wars, to stores and churches,
The market is for masses
Who buy whatever they're told,
From guns to night sunglasses.

But to make a difference,
You need a solo artist
Who sees the world uniquely
And is driven to suggest:

Out of all our numbers, none
Is stronger than a single one.

I AM TREE

There's a sign
For firewood I see.
It's not large,
But it's nailed to a tree.

Makes me think
How much I run from
Place to place,
Shut away from the sun.

My mind digs;
I sway in my boots.
How far I
Am from putting down roots.

Stand your ground
Is for the trees.
They don't shout
Or trigger shooting sprees.

Out beyond
Solidarity
I cease me.
I am free. I AM TREE!

LOVE ARMY

When violence knocks,
Why must we
Answer with blows?
Now we start
Wars over bigots,
Drugs and ideas.

Does anyone watching
See an eye
For an eye
Is blindingly myopic?
Shots returned only
Make more wounded.

Stuck in a
Bog of hatred,
Mothers in Belfast
Had the courage
To wage peace.

For every Caesar,
Let there be
One General Ghandi,
Recruiting our best
And brightest for
His love army.

UNDER THE INFLUENCE

Take all drugs that stimulate reactions,
Which serpent's fangs feel sharpest on our throats?
Granted, any substance or addiction
Can ruin lives, along with all those close.
And once we name our poison, here's the kick:
We want to know if our answer is correct.
That's when the needle sinks in nice and deep.
Think of all we do to be the right one,
Or the left, so long as we're invited
To whichever party we strive to join.
But when we feel the pressure on to please,
Consider what would happen if we said:
I am a fully developed being
With too many scars, visions and passions
To ever be under the influence
Of words, labels or restrictions again!

PART V

THE WORLD STANDS STILL

LOVE'S HERMIT

To this day, I
Still fall ill when
Cameras flash
And lenses bare.

So in the dark,
I think alone,
Assembling words
With utmost care.

My hope's grown thin
While my skin is thick,
Protecting me
From pain and stare.

But all my strength
Springs from within—
Since once in love,
Out is nowhere.

LONGHAIRED LAUGHTER

Lately, in the afternoons
When the horizon hangs
Heavy with storm clouds
Full of unsettling news,
I find myself enjoying
The companionship of
Longhaired laughter.
It nourishes, not unlike
Rest before a challenge.
It also reminds me
Why I wear a crew cut
And keep one ear
Battle ready—listening
For the coming thunder.

FEAR KNOT

It starts circling
In the head
Or the guts
Or the heart
And winds around
Itself tighter than
A towing hawser
And heavier than
An anchor chain
Forged in the
Flames of cannot.
But like any
Line, its strength
Comes from tension.
That is why
Everyday, I calmly
Strive to be
The fid in
Your fear knot.

ALL SMILES START

A skilled surgeon,
Who'd sliced and repaired all forty-three muscles
That work in unison to comprise the human face,
Couldn't say precisely how many
Were needed to create just one smile.

An esteemed psychiatrist,
Capable of rooting out the deepest seeds
Sown into the most unfathomable psyche,
Was left groping for an empiric theory
To rightfully govern the interpretation of smiles.

A renowned primatologist,
More at home in the trees than any skyscraper
And openly accepted by gorillas and orangutans,
Still had to guess on several occasions
Whether a curled lip meant friend or foe.

Yet a humble denizen,
Who's no duke with no painted duchess,
Felt commanded to draw the curtain and report:
Whether born of good or evil intent,
All smiles start from the center of the heart.

SUNS ON SAND

Whenever I meet
Somebody who brims
Full of faith,
I overflow in
Rivers of doubt.

Then there are
The flocking majorities,
Whose sure numbers
Surely leave me
Frozen in singularity.

Yet I felt
A gypsy's glance
That still warms
My heart like
Suns on sand.

A BURNING LOVE OF FROST

Go find poetry in a woodchopper's axe-handle,
he said.
Blistered hands and an aching back is all
I'd find.
Good fences make good neighbors—or so goes
his wisdom.
My neighbor's gone, and his fence fell over
in my yard.

In a yellow wood, he chose and made
a difference,
While the grassy way remains the only road
for me.
In a supporting cedar pole he saw sureness
of soul.
I read of bondage, and all I desire
is your love.

Unwilling to explain his outwalking all city lights
in rain,
I feel his dark acquaintance whenever I drop
my eyes.
When it snows, he reminds me of promises
I keep
And the deep miles I traveled to be
open for you.

Now, with hands heated by a fire that I built,
I sleep as the woodchuck, untroubled by guilt.

THE WORLD STANDS STILL

When it snows in Northern New England

She proclaims it's like the world stands

Still

Hurriedly I offer her my breathless agreement

Then quietly admire the audacity of snow's

Silence

Screaming snowmobiles snowblowers and snowplows will shatter

My reverie like boots breaking pockets of

Ice

But not before I notice the Celt

In her features and my world stands

Still

NOTES

Page 5: "Oh, Wicked One"

Hobomock: Native American for Wicked One, according to Narragansett and Wampanoag legends, an evil spirit that dwells in the jagged rocks and dark waters off the coasts of Scituate and Cohasset, Massachusetts.

Near a hundred Irish: In 1843, I.W.P. Lewis, a lighthouse inspector, submitted a report listing more than 40 vessels wrecked the previous decade upon Minot's Ledge. The worst of these tragedies involved 99 Irish immigrants from one vessel, who drowned within view of their new country.

Lover's Light: Minot's Ledge Light is nicknamed Lover's Light due to its distinctive 1 - 4 - 3 flash sequence, symbolic of the letters in the phrase, "I love you."

Page 9: "Homeless in the Metaphor"

Purple: Amherst College's colors are purple and white.

Metaphors all could see: "Education by Poetry" was a speech Robert Frost delivered at Amherst College. It was later published in the February 1931 edition of the *Amherst Graduates' Quarterly*. In it, Frost states, "What I am pointing out is that unless you are home in the metaphor, unless you have had your proper poetical education in the metaphor, you are not safe anywhere."

Page 10: "A Rail"

The Secret Annex: the hiding spot of the Frank family during World War II, where Anne Frank composed her famous diary.

Page 21: "The Goat's Song"

The Goat's Song: The Greek word "Tragoedia" literally translates as goat song. The term refers to the best dramatic performance during the ancient festival of the god Dionysus, as well as to the goat presented as the prize to the winning playwright.

Page 23: "Used Too"

Lines written early one morning in a used car parking lot.

Page 24: "The Last Strand"

Samuel Gray: A rope maker and also the first colonist shot by British soldiers on March 5, 1770, the day famously remembered as the Boston Massacre.

Page 26: "My Ríastrad"

Ríastrad: The Irish or Gaelic term for battle frenzy, the shockingly dangerous force that allowed Cú Chulainn to single-handedly stop sieges and kill hundreds, but left him terrifyingly disfigured and unable to distinguish friends from foes.

Sétanta: Cú Chulainn's birth name.

Thomas Kinsella and Ciaran Carson both translated the Irish epic the *Táin Bó Cúailnge* ("Cattle Raid of Cooley") into English.

Seanchaite: Plural form of *seanchaí,* a traditional Irish bard or storyteller.

Page 33: "You're All"

In 2011, Ellyn Ruthstrom, then President of the Bisexual Resource Center, the oldest national bi organization in the U.S., told David Tuller of *The New York Times,* "Researchers want to fit bi attraction into a little box—you have to be exactly the same, attracted to men and women, and you're bisexual. That's nonsense. What I love is that people express their bisexuality in so many different ways." (22 August, 2011)

Page 37: "Boston Bi-rish"

In 2015, Mayor Marty Walsh became the first Boston mayor in twenty years to participate in the St. Patrick's Day parade after event organizers finally allowed LGBTQ groups to march in the parade for the very first time.

Page 38: "By the Time"

In 2013, the White House invited bisexual leaders to a groundbreaking roundtable discussion of the bisexual community's issues, focusing on sobering statistics related to health disparities, workplace discrimination, domestic violence and hate crimes.

Page 44: "Native America"

Geronimo: The use of the codename "Geronimo" for the U.S. military mission to kill Osama bin Laden, as well as the target himself, enraged many Native Americans, including Geronimo's great-grandson and Vietnam War veteran Harlyn Geronimo, who wrote to the White House requesting an explanation and apology. The mission was later officially renamed.

Page 45: "The Well-Drawn Notebook Man"

Inspired by the BBC article "Why is Kim Jon-un always surrounded by people taking notes?" (24 April, 2014).

Page 46: "Ghost Army"

Inspired by the BBC article "US sends military draft notices to men born in the 1800s" (11 July, 2014).

Page 48: "I Am Tree"

Stand Your Ground: A self-defense law giving individuals the right to use deadly force to defend themselves without any requirement to evade or retreat from the situation.

Page 54: "Fear Knot"

Fid: A seaman's cone-shaped tool traditionally made out of bone or wood, used to work and hold open knots and holes in canvas.

ABOUT THE AUTHOR

Kevin Hogan is a prolific poet, *Huffington Post* blogger and human rights advocate. As a self-help author, speaker and consultant, he's also an authority on the subject of healing stigma. For years an inspiring high school English instructor, his life irrevocably changed after an international news story branded him the "Porn Star Teacher."

In addition to writing and speaking, Kevin serves on the Board of Directors of the Bisexual Resource Center, the oldest national bi-specific organization. As a member of the Bisexual Leadership Roundtable, he was invited to the White House for a historic first meeting in 2013 with the Obama administration on matters of bisexual health, inclusivity and awareness. And in 2015, he was invited back to the White House for the first Bisexual Community Policy Briefing. Currently, he's also part of a working party for the U.S. Department of Health and Human Services' team Building Resilient Communities Through Trauma-Informed Congregations.

In moments of selfish bliss, Kevin enjoys long walks on the beach with his wife and their two dogs.

This book is set in Garamond Premier Pro, which had its genesis in 1988 when type-designer Robert Slimbach visited the Plantin-Moretus Museum in Antwerp, Belgium, to study its collection of Claude Garamond's metal punches and typefaces. During the mid-fifteen hundreds, Garamond—a Parisian punch-cutter—produced a refined array of book types that combined an unprecedented degree of balance and elegance, for centuries stan ding as the pinnacle of beauty and practicality in type-founding. Slimbach has created an entirely new interpretation based on Garamond's designs and on compatible italics cut by Robert Granjon, Garamond's contemporary. Titles are set in Perpetua Titling, a variant of the font designed by Eric Gill, whose work as a stone mason led to the clean lines of Perpetua.

To order additional copies of this book
or other Antrim House titles, contact the publisher at

Antrim House
21 Goodrich Rd., Simsbury, CT 06070
860.217.0023, AntrimHouse@comcast.net
or the house website (www.AntrimHouseBooks.com).

•

On the house website
in addition to information on books
you will find sample poems, upcoming events,
and a "seminar room" featuring supplemental biography,
notes, images, poems, reviews, and
writing suggestions.